What's That Daddy?

AUTHOR
ADIL ISMAEEL

ILLUSTRATOR
YAQIYN ABDUL-ZAHIR

In the name of Allah,
The Most Gracious, The Most Merciful!

Laith was growing into a curious boy who loved learning new things.

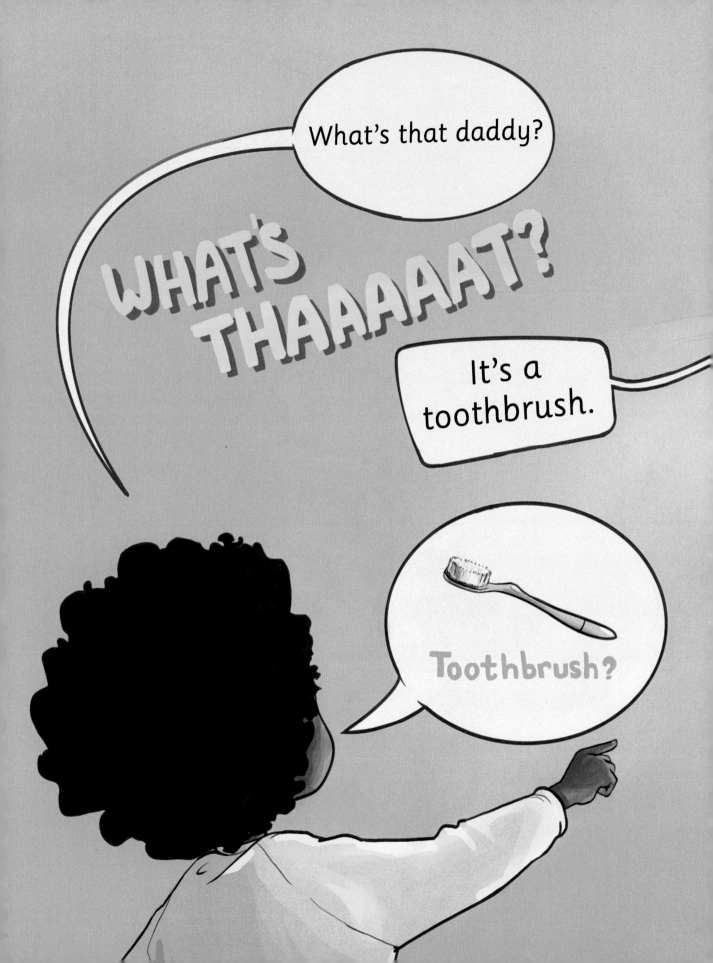

WHAT'S THAAAAAAT?

Yes, a sink is a place for running water.
You can use a sink to make wudu, wash your hands, dishes, brush your teeth or other things that need to be cleaned.

What's that daddy?

WHAT'S THAAAAAAT?

It's a toilet.

Yes, a toilet. A toilet is something you poop poop and pee pee in!

So the next time you have to poop and pee, make sure you make it to the toilet!

Brush

Yes, a brush.
A brush is used to
help fix, groom,
and style hair.

Laith looked out the window and shouted,

WHAT'S THAAAAAAT?

Yes, a tree.
Trees make shade,
oxygen, and the wood
from trees can be used
to build things.

Laith looked up at the clock.
What's that daddy?
BEEP
BEEP
8:00
WHAT'S THAAAAAAT?

While ironing his clothes, Laith's father quickly forgot about the toast in the toaster. The toast burned and started to smoke. The smoke set off the smoke detector and made a lot of noise.

Oh no!

Laith's father yelled!

As they were getting ready to leave, Laith's father picked up his keys.

PAT
PAT

Oh no!
Where's my wallet?
We're going to be late!

WHAT'S THAAAAAAT?

A wallet is something you use to carry paper money, cards, and other important documents. My wallet is brown.
Now where is it?

Laith's father looked all over for his wallet.

He thought he put it next to his keys, but it was nowhere to be found.

Laith walked over to his toy bin.
He pulled out his favorite dinosaur.

Brown?

Yes,
Brown like your
Triceratops.

Laith dug into the bin again
and pulled out something else.

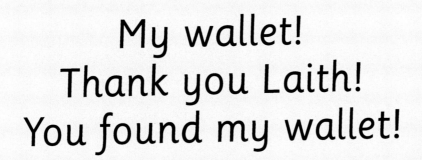

My wallet!
Thank you Laith!
You found my wallet!

Laith's father
cheered.

The End!

Made in the USA
Columbia, SC
19 December 2022

74608101R00022